A Guide To Stress-Free
Data Protection Impact
Assessments

Deborah Bowers

A Guide to Stress-Free Data Protection Impact Assessments

First edition published by self- published Author, Deborah Bowers.

The rights of the author to be identified as the author of this work has been asserted in accordance with the Copyright, Design and Patents Act 1988.

Copyright © 2019 Deborah Bowers.
ISBN: 9780992649371

Published by self-published author Deborah Bowers. Persons wishing to contact the Author may do so by emailing: justlifeevents2@gmail.com

Dedication

We are at the turn of a century and the beginning of a new age in technology. Just as Thomas Edison stood at the end of his era and the beginning of the electrical revolution, we are experiencing a similar transition. This book is dedicated to all the young bright minds who are driving this digital revolution and moving us forward to the next phase.

Why Read This Guide

Most books on this subject have been written by experts who have concerned themselves with legal interpretations and complex arguments as to how legal challenges or interpretations may be determined. This guide is written from a practical standpoint, the author being a Solicitor of England and Wales, who has worked within the telecommunications and technology sector for the past 4 years, as at the date of publication of this guide. In this guide, I seek to set aside the legal analyses. Instead, I have sought to build a bridge between the legal considerations, the technical considerations and the cybersecurity concerns required when conducting an effective Data Protection Impact Assessment; also referred to as privacy assessments. These terms will be used interchangeably throughout this guide as well as the abbreviation (DPIA).

Privacy assessments are one of the few fields where it helps to have an understanding of the language of law, cyber security, and digital engineering. An understanding of the language of all 3 disciplines is critical to a harmonious working environment, as the language of each disciple cuts across this area of work. It is a breath of fresh air to any expert when he or she finds that the person with whom he or she is speaking, speaks or understands his or her language.

This book is written with telecommunications and technology companies in mind. This does not exclude the use of this guide by other persons, but the examples which will be used here are those which can be found in the telecommunications and technology sector. As with any industry where a data protection impact assessment is being conducted, it helps to understand the language of the sector.

Within the telecommunications sector one will be speaking of APIs, AWS, DIA NBIA, WAN. LAN, WLAN amongst other technical terms. The Cyber Security expert on the other hand will be concerned with trojans, worms, authentication, and malware. The legal mind will be attentive to the overlaps between various industry standards such as standards relating to the processing of financial data, binding corporate rules, cookie policies, privacy notices, compliance with the Data Protection Act 2018, the Privacy of Electronic Communications Regulations 2003, with its amendments and other regulatory requirements. Of equal importance when dealing with telecommunication and technology companies is the Network and Infrastructure Systems Regulations (NIS Regulations). The concern here, of the legal expert, will be to ensure compliance with the law, whilst at the same time, protecting the client from breach thereof.

I have done my best to shy away from the complications which each of these areas in their own right pose and focus instead on the physical process, the people involved and what they bring to the table. I have also sought to identify synergies which can easily be overlooked when carrying out an assessment. This is because a data protection impact assessment is more than a data gathering exercise. The information gathered is vital to the determination of risk and to the demonstration of accountability and compliance by the organisation.

However, in writing this guide I have taken for granted that the reader will have some knowledge of Data Protection Impact Assessments and the associated legislation. I do not seek to teach those who are unfamiliar with the ropes, the process, but this book can serve as an excellent guide to anyone who is embarking upon this area of work as far as the practical aspects are concerned. The new student will need however to read through the relevant legislation to uncover the requirements and will not be able to rely on this guide to get to the heart of regulatory obligations and compliance.

TABLE OF CONTENTS

CHAPTER 1

WHY ALL THE FUSS?

Establishing Ownership, Roles and Responsibilities

The internet is here to stay and our use of it is only likely to increase as the post internet generation gives way to millennials, those born using the Internet as a necessary and daily part of their everyday life. This inevitable expansion in the use of the Internet, to access goods and services, such as shopping, paying bills, accessing information and in the provision of security management, amongst other things has sparked off the debate as to who owns the information which is being uploaded onto the internet on a daily basis. The uploading of such information is essential as it facilitates our participation in the benefits provided by the Internet. There is also the increasing use of data for analytics. One recalls only too clearly the American Presidential Elections scandal, which resulted in the election of Donald Trump as president and the alleged exploitation of data from Facebook by the Russians and Cambridge Analytica.

It has become important to establish ownership of the data freely provided by us all onto the Internet. The European Commission has also seen it fit to allocate roles and responsibilities to those who collect, control or process data. Express consent to use data needs to be provided save for in circumstances where some other legitimate use of the data can be established. Provisions have also been made to ensure that one knows where that data is being stored or transferred to, if transferred outside the EU and the measures in place to protect or secure such data. In our everchanging world where cyber security is the new frontline, safe storage of data has taken centre stage. Standards have been set, to ensure that the environments within which data is being stored outside the EU and within the EU complies with essential standards of cyber security, once that data relates to a European national, now commonly referred to as a data subject.

The data subject has been given centre stage and consequences are to be imposed where the rights of the data subject have been breached. Where there is no punishment for an act, it may be said that no wrong has been committed. That being said this is certainly not the case in relation to data protection within the EU. Supervisory Authorities have been established in all EU territories to oversee, enforcement of the GDPR. They have also been given extensive powers to penalize those who dare to breach the rules with fines more excruciating than the sting of a scorpion. Fines have been set at up to 2% of gross worldwide revenue or €10,000,000.00 whichever is the greater, for administrative wrongs and up to 20% of gross annual turnover or €20,000,000.00, or the greater thereof, for other infringements. Such fines are intended to stir all towards compliance. Not getting this right could signal sudden death to the continued viability of any enterprise should a fine at the highest level be imposed.

Taking Pre-emptive Action.

In this brave new world of the Internet, it would be fool hardy to ignore the dangers posed by its use. The Internet represents as great a threat to our way of living, of equal proportion to the benefits which it provides, should it be manipulated by those with malicious intent. Today we can track the whereabouts of persons using GPS technology which can easily be installed in watches, bags, phones etc. Although we welcome this technology for example when used to keep our children safe, or to help us remember where we parked our vehicle, it can also be used to our detriment, by those with criminal intent.

We now face the danger of our personal information being more accessible. Our financial data can be accessed without executing a bank robbery in the traditional sense depriving us of our financial assets. Our biological data can also be used to arrive at decisions which discriminate against or in favour of persons of different ethnic groups.

Personal data has become a trading commodity. New businesses often purchase lists giving them the names and addresses of potential customers. The "List" enables them to acquire new customers, without the knowledge or consent of these customers. Such liberties have been greatly curtailed by the GDPR and the Data Protection Act 1998, which has incorporated the GDPR. When we buy goods and services using online platforms, we upload our personal information online which may be accessed by someone skilled in the art of hacking. This information may then be sold to others who may access your bank account or purchase goods and services using your financial data. It is therefore necessary to protect not only your personal information but to impose standards of cyber security on those who collect and process your details online, rendering it vulnerable to hackers.

Cyber warfare is the new art of warfare, which we must all guard against. Our security depends on it. Our children may in the future be more knowledgeable about cyber security risk, but the onus is upon us right now to educate ourselves about it and put in place standards, which will enable us to protect ourselves.

In light of these many benefits and challenges which we now face online, the GDPR or General Data Protection Regulations is intended to provide clarity as to what is personal data, who does it belong to, our rights and obligations in relation to the personal information which we provide, to companies both online and offline.

As this book is written with telecommunication and technology companies in mind it would be remiss of me to make no mention of the Privacy of Electronic Communications Regulations or (PECR), which came into effect on 8th May 2018. Little mention has been made of it, unlike the GDPR, possibly because it does not carry the daunting fines associated with breaches of the GDPR. However, they are of no less importance. The PECR and the obligations which it creates will therefore be discussed in conjunction with the GDPR, as it provides additional obligations for consideration and implementation by technology and telecommunications providers.

CHAPTER 2

THE GDPR/DATA PROTECTION ACT 2018

The GDPR came into force on 25th May 2018, throughout the European Community. In the UK the Data Protection Act 2018, came into effect at the same time and sought to embrace legislation pertaining to personal data, access to information, amongst other things.

In compliance with the GDPR all organisations in Europe, which are part of the European Community umbrella, will need to pay closer attention to how personal data is obtained , and utilised, as specific consent is required to ensure that data has been obtained with the explicit consent of the owner, unless there is some other legitimate purpose which would justify accessing and utilising that individual's data. Further, the legislation seeks to monitor whether any personal data obtained from individuals commonly referred to as the "data subjects" is utilised only for the purposes for which the "data subject" gave it. As the legislation only applies to living persons, wherever the word "data subject" is used it is referring to a living being.

Organisations also need to demonstrate that they can protect the data which they collect, process or store. They are required to carry out Data Privacy Impact Assessments (DPIA) to guide them as to the possible risk to data subjects, should their data fall into the wrong hands. The need for a DPIA, is to be evaluated at the beginning of any project or at the point at which a new product or service is considered. This is described as privacy by design and ensures that privacy and data protection is considered at the very outset of any product or service under consideration. In circumstances where such considerations have never been taken into account or are in need of review, organisations are to be undertake the same for all products and services utilising personal data. This approach helps to demonstrate compliance should anything go wrong which triggers an Information Commission Investigation. It is the completing of this Data Protection Impact Assessment, which has become a monster in the minds of many employees.

The main contact person for the development and oversite of the Data Privacy Impact Assessment is the Data Protection Officer, (DPO), who relies upon the expertise of staff and any third parties involved in the process. The DPO should be involved in the entire processes from beginning to end. Where the process has commenced prior to the appointment of a DPO, the DPO should be made aware and get involved as early as possible.

Each company need not have its own DPO as the legislation does not exclude sharing. However, the role of the DPO is to understand and know the working and the application of the

GDPR as an expert and to assist the organisation in implementing its requirements. The DPO is also required to remain in contact with the regulatory authority and to advise on how best to protect customers or clients in the unlikely event of a data breach.

The ability to advise and guidance others on the requirements of the GDPR is fundamental to the role. The training of executives and employees is also within the remit of the DPO, ensuring that their level of knowledge demonstrates an appreciation for the required so that they are able to understand and apply, their knowledge to their responsibilities under the GDPR.

A major role of the Data Protection Officer is to assist the organisation in assessing risk. The level of risk to which a data subject is likely to be exposed should their data be compromised. The Data Privacy Assessment is designed as a framework or tool to help evaluate the risk. Many have found this process daunting with its many questions and need for specific considerations. This book sets out to make light or to iron out the process for all readers, rendering it stress-free.

CHAPTER 3

GETTING STARTED

Creating awareness

Many companies have focused their in-house training around the General Data Protection Regulations as a whole enabling staff to understand what is meant by personal data, the requirements of the regulations which are now legislation as of 25th May 2018. Such training is essential as it explains the rights of "data subjects" (i.e. living human beings, under the legislation). It also high lights the fines and brings home just how important compliance is to the organisation. However, during the course of educating staff little emphasis is placed on the Data Protection Impact Assessment. Discussion about this assessment is kept to a minimal so as not to confuse staff who are coming to grips with the many new concepts introduced by the legislation. The detail which relates to the Data Protection Impact Assessment is left to the Data Protection Officer to master and guide the organisation.

However, I have found that despite undertaking General Data Protection training, many members of the technical team, who are at the forefront the daily flow of data, had little knowledge of the requirements of a Data Protection

Impact and Assessment and what it sought to achieve for the organisation. More often than not the technical experts were reluctant to say too much about the flow of the data or where it was being stored or transferred, or the level of support provided by various organisations which were involved in the handling of the data. Neither were they able to readily appreciate that the flow or exchange of data between servers all be it that it the data was not being stored in the device raised security risk.

It is therefore of paramount importance that organisations educate their staff not only generally in relation to the what the GDPR entails in very limited detail but also specifically sets up a programme for its technical staff who would generally be expected to assist with the completion of Data Privacy Impact Assessments. They should be educated as to the types of data which is being processed and captured, in relation to the GDPR as well as the Privacy of Electronic Communication Regulations and other provisions which seek to protect the security of data and to assess the risk to individual of that data being accessed, altered or lost.

Purpose of the DPIA.

The DPIA is a document intended to evaluate risk and put in place a strategy to deal with it. It Is therefore important that there exist a clear plan or strategy for carrying out the DPIA. The products, services and processes which the organisation provides should be identified and the relevant persons required to carry out the DPIA should all be readily available. For example, the DPO may require a project manager to oversee the flow of the work and compliance with deadlines, further access to the technical team should be secured such as, access to the data architect who has designed the product process or service, a member of the technical team who understands the data flow, a member of the service staff who use the system on a daily basis and knows exactly what data is requested for each service.

The GDPR requires organisation to acquire only as much data as is required to provide the product or service. The customer support teams, who are usually the ones requesting the data necessary to open an account or ensure compliance with the requirements of the organisation are best placed to identify what data if any is being collected which is not essential to the provision of the product, process or service.

The organisation also needs to determine how the DPIA is to be carried out and provide guidance as to methods which may be adopted, such as the holding of public consultations, reviewing suppliers, reviewing storage arrangements for cloud-based services, contacting data subjects or whether the process should be merely an internal process or otherwise.

CHAPTER 4

WHAT ARE WE TO CAPTURE?

The DPIA is designed to account for the personal data, collected or processed by a Controller or Data Processor and document what information is being collected, why it is being collected, any relevant consents or legitimate purposes, it's movement, the systems through which it is processed, where it is stored, and the persons who may have access to it. It is advisable here to explain this reference to Controllers and Data Processors.

Controllers are persons who dictate what information is to be collected and how the information is to be used. A Data Processor takes instructions from the Controller as to how the information is to be manipulated. Determining at what stage of the processes a party is acting as a Controller or Processor of information can sometimes prove tricky and so the law has set out some parameters when it is to be assumed that the person within a particular role will be acting as either a Controller or processor of personal data.

The bigger question is what are we to capture which is or may be deemed to be personal data? The answer to this question is dependent upon the type of industry which you are operating in. In this guide I will be looking at the type of information which technology and telecommunications companies may capture.

In any event, when collecting personal data, it is advisable to divide the data collected into categories of data. This will help you focus on the specific area that you are considering until you move on to the next category. Here is an example of some data categories:

1. **Account data** / Customer data – this relates to the information you gather from customers to open their account. Some examples are: name, address, post code, telephone number, email address, suffix, Mr, Mrs, Miss, date of birth, gender, marital status, age, etc

2. **Employee data**: name, address, profile picture, marital status, next of kin, children, qualifications, training record, performance appraisals, disciplinary records, complaints, redundancy record, general correspondence, user name and password, record of internal investigations, attendance record, health and wellness record, medical reports, accident reports, copy of signature, health questionnaires, biometric records such as voice samples, fingerprints, palm print retina scans, IP address, Mac address, other unique identifiers, etc

3. **Supplier data:** name and address, details of employees or contact persons, telephone number, email, bank details, copy of supplier's passport or ID, copy of signature, licences held, operating system, network, based location, devise based location, CCTV, monitoring of calls, monitoring of entry and exit, monitoring of browsing etc.

4. **Electronic data:** Cookies, IP address, geographical data, location data, such as GPS, etc. An understanding of PECR will enable the DPO to determine what further areas need to be included here if any.

5. **Sensitive data**: race, religion, political affiliation, memberships, for example trade union membership, mental history, medical history etc.

CHAPTER 5

70 KEY CONSIDERATIONS FOR THE DATA PROTECTION OFFICER

Now that the data being collected has been set-out, it is now for the DPO to consider some key questions, which will need to be addressed when the data is considered as part of the DPIA process. These considerations are essential to ensure compliance with legislative requirements.

1. Why is the data being collected?
2. Who is carrying out the assessment?
3. Date of the assessment.
4. Who is the Privacy Officer?
5. Who is the Security Officer?
6. What is the name of the Data architect?
7. What is the name of the product manager or business owner?
8. Is the collection of this data necessary for providing the goods or service?
9. Is this data required to enable the billing team to carry out its functions?
10. Is this information required for authentication of the customer's subscription?

11. Is the information used to identify the customer?
12. Is the customer's information used for marketing purposes? If "YES" Has the customer consented to such use?
13. Is there proof of such consent? Where can this proof be found? In what format is it?
14. Is a CSV format available in the event of the customer making a request for that information?
15. Is the information collected used for analytics?
16. How long is the information kept for?
17. Who is it shared with? Has the customer consented?
18. Has the customer been provided with a Privacy Policy? Where is this policy made available to the customer? At what point of the customer's interaction with the company is this policy made available to the customer?
19. Does any of this data relate to children? If yes how old are they? Has the consent of their parent/ guardian been obtained?
20. Does any of this data relate to persons who are vulnerable or disabled?
21. In light of the product or service being offered is the requested information necessary?. Does the product or service result in discrimination due to automation of results?
22. Is communications content being processed?
23. Where you are dealing with communications content is this as a result of deep packet inspection, (which is forbidden save for limited circumstances) or

24. Is it as a result of a service being offered to the customer at the customer's request such as s voicemail?
25. Does the service include location data, GPS or otherwise, which can be obtained from the customer's device?
26. Can the Customer's device be accessed unknown to the customer?
27. Is any information being gathered from the customer's device?
28. Has any sensitive information been collected, such as the customers sexual orientation, race, political opinions etc?
29. Was it necessary to collect such information to provide the goods or service?
30. How is the information collected at #19 being preserved to ensure its privacy?
31. Are customers able to exercise control over the data which has been collected about them?
32. Has any financial data been collected?
33. Where financial data has been collected have the industry codes of conduct in relation to such data been complied with?
34. Where is the data being stored?
35. What systems are they being stored in?
36. Where are those systems located?
37. If in the UK, do they meet standards of cybersecurity?
38. If stored outside the UK, do they pass the standards set by the European union and have the approval of the Supervisory Authority approval? How easily might

this data be retrieved should there be a issue with the storage company such as bankruptcy or should the data be required for legal proceedings?

39. What agreements are in place to provide clarity as to the roles and responsibilities of all parties?.
40. What suppliers do you work with?
41. What information is being shared with them?
42. Are suppliers GDPR and Cyber Security compliant?
43. Has the supplier's staff been trained and are they fully aware of the risk posed by breaches?
44. Are there any cross-border data transfer and privacy considerations, such as shields? Is the country one, which is considered as having adequate security, are any binding Corporate Rules necessary?
45. How long is the data to be stored for?
46. What areas will require remediation?
47. What clarifications may be required from the legal team, the security or privacy team or any other source?
48. What are the gaps as they relate to the legislation?
49. Where will remediation be required?
50. Is there a remediation process in place?
51. Where has the remediation process been documented?
52. Who is responsible for each aspect of the remediation?
53. Have clear deadlines been set to complete remediation?
54. How are those deadlines being monitored?

55. Has a data map or flowchart in relation to the data been created?
56. Has the graphics expert been notified of who the best contact person is in relation to the data flow?
57. Who is the point of contact for each area of responsibility?
58. Is there any area where advice from the ICO may be required?
59. Do the NIS Regulations apply?
60. Are any restricted transfers involved?
61. Is the country to which the information is being transferred Iceland, Norway or Liechtenstein to which the GDPR applies based on the EEA Joint Committee decision in relation to those countries?
62. Is the transfer to any of the following countries? Austria, Belgium, Bulgaria, Croatia, Cyprus, Czech Republic, Denmark, Estonia, Finland, France, Germany, Greece, Hungary, Ireland, Italy, Latvia, Lithuania, Luxembourg, Malta, Netherlands, Poland, Portugal, Romania, Slovakia, Slovenia, Spain, Sweden and the United Kingdom.
63. Will binding corporate rules agreements be required?
64. Is this a transfer between two public authorities where a contract is required?
65. Has the Commission made a full finding of adequacy in relation to the country where the data is to be transferred?
66. Does the EU-US privacy shield framework apply?
67. Does the company hold a certificate for the type of data being transferred?

68. What standards of privacy and security have been complied with? Are those standards recognised by the European Commission as adequate?
69. What are some of the standards which would be applicable to this data?
70. Is there anything which should be brought to the attention of the ICO?

CHAPTER 6

WHO SHOULD BE INVOLVED

Getting the right people involved in the carrying out of a data protection impact assessment is vital to a stress-free process. Of the hundred or so DPIAs which I have conducted I found very few people who understood what my role was or what was to be achieved from the process. There is always the one in fifty persons who is willing to volunteers to assist me is inspired by the process. This has always proven indispensable, as to most persons participating in a data protection impact assessment it is one of the most boring and tedious activities to be undertaken, within the spectrum of their work. Here is a list of persons whom I have found useful, during the course of my work within the technology and telecommunications sector.

Digital Engineers

Experience in this field has led me to believe that the engineers are the real heroes in this process, without sideling the contribution of the cyber security teams. The value of an engineer who knows the equipment inside out, what the equipment is capable of and who is able to carefully explain to you these functions is invaluable.

Data mapping team

The engineer is also valuable to the data mapping team. The role of the data mapping team is to demonstrate by way of a diagram exactly how the data flows. Producing a data map or data flow diagram is an essential requirement of the DPIA process.

Customer service staff

Another group of persons who should not be overlooked are the customer service staff and billing staff, who are able to take you through what information is needed to carry out a service or in relation to a product. They are usually surprised when they are called upon to explain what they do and why they need the information which is being gathered. They are the ones who interact with the customers and are able to deal with the nuances which may arise during the course of a call or whist providing a service. They are able to remember that the customer during the course of the conversation may give information which amounts to personal information which is recorded and stored in the company's data base. Such information may or may not be relevant to obtaining the service. Such revelations alert the Data Protection Office of need to ensure that such recordings are redacted thus ensuring compliance with regulatory requirements.

Graphic designers

The graphic designers should be a member of the data mapping team, able to represent the data flow, which is an essential part of the DPIA process. It is therefore essential that they have an understanding of how the data flows, to effectively represent this as a data map.

Departmental Mangers

Managers are able to alert the Data Protection Officer, or the assessor of third-party organisations engaged in data processing activities, which may not have been hi-lighted at the outset. For example, organisations, providing redacting services to ensure that stored data does not contain irrelevant personal information about the customer or information which breaches regulatory and industry standards. Managers are often able to identify the best contact person or department with the knowledge needed to address a challenge encountered during the process. This may be because they are quick to extricate themselves from any work which does not involve their department or their staff, whatever their reasons. They will be sure to provide some guidance as to your next port of call.

Support staff

A group of persons who are often forgotten are the lines of support. Some companies provided first, second and third line support which may be farmed out to third parties. All these persons may at some point be given some information pertaining to the customer. It is vital that these lines of support are identified during the assessment and what information if any is shared with them, to enable them to carry out their functions.

Where products are sold to various enterprises, it should not be assumed that everything is identical as to their administration, further questions about billing teams, storage, and lines of support may surprise you. It is advisable to ask further questions in relation to these.

Remediation team

I dare not forget the remediation team whose responsibility it is to follow up with the various departments, comprising cyber security experts, privacy experts and the product team, to ensure that updates and gaps identified as requiring remediation are addressed. A progress map is also vital to enable the organisation to keep abreast with its progress. This also renders the organisation more accountable should any questions be asked of it by the regulatory authority.

Project managers

Let us not forget the project managers whose responsibility it is to crack the whip and keep the project on budget and ensure that all teams are meeting the deliverables. It is vital that everyone understands the contribution they make to the process as each input is vital to the success of the assessment and the evaluation of present and future risk.

Legal team

The legal team has a vital role to play to ensure compliance with the various regulatory requirements. The GDPR, the PECR, and within the contractual context, consideration needs to be given to the relevant terms and conditions when engaging third parties. Most relevant being compliance with the GDPR and PECR, as well as ISO standards of security and privacy. Further the importance of indemnity clauses in all contract, in the event that they may fall foul of the GDPR bringing the organisation into disrepute. Binding Corporate Rules and agreements should be carefully drafted to protect the organisation. Cookie policies, privacy and security policies and terms and conditions all need to be updated, clearly written, providing users with all relevant information to make informed decisions.

The team needs to mindful of timeframes for responding to request for information and data breaches. The status of the organisation and any additional roles and responsibilities which it may need to comply with as a result of its status. Compliance with any NIS regulations is also essential such as operators of essential services and digital service providers such as cloud based services. It is easy to forget the NIS Regulations, which relate to those who provide essential services and relevant digital service providers. There are more stringent rules which apply to them, as the value of the services which they provide if tampered with can impact national security.

Privacy and security team

This is where the heavy lifting takes place. Once the gap has been identified it is for this team to find the solution, where it is within their ability or having received the solution from another team such as the legal team to put it into its proper place.

CHAPTER 7

PRIVACY & SECURITY

Privacy and security, have now become bedfellows due to the risk to personal data, inherent in the use of the Internet. Businesses use the Internet to market goods and services. They use email, telephone, text, and fax marketing, a trend which has grown as businesses continue to use electronic communications to reach customers. Some examples are opt-in pages and landing pages which require customers to provide a name, email and sometimes a telephone contact. Companies also use Cookies to track the activities of customers when they use their websites. This information can be used for analytics, to understand the choices and needs of customers. Electronic equipment is capable of locating customers, through GPS tracking, IP addresses etc.

People have now been given specific privacy rights in relation to the use of their data for automated telephone calls and more physical means such as direct marketing. It was common practice for companies to purchase "Lists" containing the names and addresses of customers, and contact these unsuspecting customers, who often wondered how their information has been obtained. Consent is now required for such activities where the customers personal information is being used such as their name. Companies who contact customers via phone services are required to display their number.

A common definition of consent has been adopted under the GDPR/ Data Protection Act 2018, and PECR. This consent must be given, willingly, and must be expressly given.

Of great importance is the obligation placed upon organisations to keep personal information safe. The NIS Regulation 2018 is designed to impose high levels of security systems. Greater emphasis is placed upon Network and Service Providers complying with article 95 of the PECR as this would render them in compliance with the GDPR and the relevant provisions under the Data Protection Act 2018.

Networks or Service Providers, only need to comply with PECR rules on:

- security and security breaches;
- traffic data;
- location data;
- itemised billing; and
- line identification services.

However, consideration needs to be given as to whether compliance is required with NIS Regulations, based on the size of the organisation, as having 50 staff or more and an annual turnover of €10 million.

The overlap

All three pieces of legislation, the Data protection Act and the PECR and the NIS Regulation play a major role and are essential considerations. Whilst the Data Protection Act 2018, the GDPR and the PECR seek to protect the personal data of EU Citizens globally. The NIS regulations seek to protect the systems which store such data.

The mayor overlap is between the DPA and the PECR. They apply to the data of living persons. The PECR deviates slightly at this juncture as it also applies to company data. The NIS sets the standards of cyber security to be applied to the systems which house data.

The ICO has power to address breaches in relation to all three pieces of legislation.

Breach of PECR carries a fine of up to £500,000.00. Despite this fine not being as severe as those embodied within the GDPR the Data Protection Act, they are significant enough to cause companies to pay attention. Firms can face criminal prosecution, non-criminal enforcement and audits from the ICO for breach of PECR.

Breach of the Data Protection Act 2018, or the GDPR is addressed by the ICO as discussed earlier in this guide. Compliance with The Network and Information Systems

(Amendment) Regulations 2018, should not be overlooked, which also falls within the remit of the ICO. They introduce standard of security for organisations which are deemed to be likely targets of cyberattacks, the result of which could undermine national security.

Breach of the NIS Regulations as they relate to relevant digital service providers may activate enforcement notices and powers of inspection or the imposition of a fine of up to £17 million by the ICO. Care should be taken however, to understand the role of the ICO as it applies to relevant digital services operators as opposes to operators of essential services. The ICO is not directly responsible for breaches by operators of essential services, but its powers are triggered where the operator of essential services also processes personal data, which falls within its remit.

Useful References:

ICO website: www.ico.org.uk

PECR: https://ico.org.uk/for-organisations/guide-to-pecr/

National cyber security centre (NCSC) www.ncsc.gov.uk

https://ec.europa.eu/info/law/law-topic/data-protection_en

https://gdpr-info.eu

Data Protection Act 2018- https://ico.org.uk/for-organisations/data-protection-act-2018/

Binding Corporate Rules: https://ico.org.uk/media/for-organisations/documents/2259711/wp-256-bcr-controllers-referential.pdf

https://ico.org.uk/media/for-organisations/documents/2259555/wp263-rev01-co-operation-procedure.pdf

- **International data transfers using model contracts:** https://ec.europa.eu/info/law/law-topic/data-protection/data-transfers-outside-eu/model-contracts-transfer-personal-data-third-countries_en

- Working Document setting up a table with the elements and principles to be found in Processor Binding Corporate Rules, updated 29th November 2017

- Data Protection Impact Assessments: https://ico.org.uk/for-organisations/guide-to-the-general-data-protection-regulation-gdpr/data-protection-impact-assessments-dpias/

- REGULATION (EU) 2016/679 OF THE EUROPEAN PARLIAMENT AND OF THE COUNCIL of 27 April 2016: https://eur-lex.europa.eu/legal-content/EN/TXT/PDF/?uri=CELEX:32016R0679&from=EN

- The European Data Protection Board: Guidelines on Data Protection Impact Assessment (DPIA) and determining whether processing is "likely to result in a high risk" for the purposes of Regulation 2016/679

- Countries affected by the GDPR

- Austria
- Belgium
- Bulgaria
- Croatia
- Republic of Cyprus
- Czech Republic
- Denmark
- Estonia
- Finland
- France
- Germany
- Greece

- Hungary
- Ireland
- Italy
- Latvia
- Lithuania
- Luxembourg
- Malta
- Netherlands
- Poland
- Portugal
- Romania
- Slovakia
- Slovenia
- Spain
- Sweden
- United Kingdom- UK has passes the Data Protection Act 2018, which has incorporated the GDPR principles and requirements into UK law. This legislation will remain applicable even after Brexit.

The End

Printed in Great Britain
by Amazon

22560609R00030